Solace Through Writing

A Calendar Journal

to use when you are beset by grief

Introduction

Did You Know How Much I Loved You?

Every day we live can be considered a juncture in our lives. One of these junctures is experiencing grief, and, when grief strikes us, we often find that the loss of someone we have loved questions our very purpose in life. The world can seem impossibly lonely and we are stricken to our very core.

When we lose someone we love, we also find that the world has expectations of us. Thus, during the turmoil and heartbreak of our grief, we have one important decision to make—how will we manage the grief?

Many of us have discovered that understanding and living through grief is a process that is much like the waters on a beach, ebbing and flowing. Some days are better than others and some days are just too difficult to deal with at that moment. We learn to understand and accept that.

There are no magical words to guarantee comfort; however, many have found that writing their thoughts helps to acknowledge their emotions, finding solace through thoughtful reflection. Keeping a journal through this journey also offers a way to honor the one we have loved.

This journal is designed to help you frame your thoughts. Some days you may write only one word—such as "Empty"—because that is how you feel at that moment. On other days you may be ready to tell a story, recall specific memories, or speak directly of your sorrow. Consider keeping this journal as a gift to yourself.

To help you when you can't always think of something to write, prompts have been provided that may help you begin to make sense of your loss or focus on a specific topic. You need not follow these prompts, but consider them as nudges from your heart.

The process of grief is generally viewed as stages that the bereaved person works through. This will not be exactly the same for everyone, but realizing that there are stages of bereavement may help you frame your feelings, your thoughts, and the reactions you have toward all you will experience during the first year of your loss.

Above all, remember that grieving doesn't follow a schedule. It lingers for years, hitting us sometimes when we least expect it. Friends come and go, you will grow in your understanding, and whatever you decide to do, life around you will go on. We hope you find some of these meditations helpful as you continue your quest for understanding what you are experiencing. These reflections may direct your thoughts, comfort you, and support your passage to rediscovering yourself as you go forward while honoring the memory of the one you have loved and lost.

About the Author

Michele DeRosa has been counseling families through the process of grieving for more than thirty years and has created countless individualized memorial services. Her kindness, skill, empathy, and unaffected love are widely known among the families who find guidance under her care.

Michele holds an earned degree in psychology from Millersville University in Pennsylvania as well as a degree from the Cincinnati College of Mortuary Science after being graduated from the University of Cincinnati in 1978. She is also a certified celebrant, guiding families who prefer alternative approaches to clergy-based services.

She has presented at national conferences on various educational topics and as part of a death and dying course at Buchanan Elementary School in Lancaster, Pennsylvania. Viewers may remember her from her appearance on ABC's 20/20 which featured her work with children.

A Licensed Funeral Director since 1980, she has served in numerous roles beginning with internships, management, and supervisor titles with Funeral Homes in Pennsylvania and Ohio.

Dedication

Mark Ebersole

Dr. Judith T. Witmer

Clifford Luke Hammoor

and the wonderful family and friends I am blessed to have in my life.

This book is dedicated to those acknowledged above, but especially to my dear friend, Mark Ebersole, whose death in 2001 taught me how to heal through the choices I needed to make each day.

I will always have him in my heart.

Acknowledgement

The words, stories, and thoughts expressed in this book are inspired by the love from my family, treasured friends, colleagues, mentors, and especially by the families I have been honored to counsel and admire over many years.

About the Artist

Clifford Luke Hammoor is a young artist from Southeast Indiana. Clifford is a student at the University of Cincinnati's School of Design, Architecture, Art, and Planning (DAAP) where he focuses on Industrial Design.

The Seahorse

Solace Through Writing

ISBN 978-0-9837768-6-4

EIN 26-3987880

Copyright 2015 by Yesteryear Publishing

All rights reserved. No part of this publication may be reproduced or transmitted in any form or by any means electronic or mechanical, including photocopy, recording, or any information storage and retrieval system now known or to be invented, without permission in writing from the publisher, except by a reviewer who wishes to quote brief passages in connection with a review written for inclusion in a magazine, newspaper, or broadcast.

Published in the United States by Yesteryear Publishing.

Books are available at www.amazon.com as well as through the author: mderosa@yahoo.com

Yesteryear Publishing
P.O. Box 311
Hummelstown, PA 17036
www.yesteryearpublishing.com
yesteryearpublishing@gmail.com
717-566-8655
Editor: Judith T. Witmer, EdD.
Page Designer: E. Nan Edmunds

The Seahorse

Several years ago, our company hired a consultant to create mid-management positions among our staff. It was this person—we will call her Marie—who shared a story with me, an experience that has framed my own outlook on life.

Marie told me that her husband was planning a business trip to a tropical island and invited her to join him with the plan for the two of them to spend their evenings together. Each night, he ended up being more involved with the business part of the trip than expected and Marie found herself alone. The night before they were scheduled to leave, her husband promised a quiet, romantic dinner along the beach. She waited—and waited—but the plans never materialized.

As Marie sat waiting for dinner, she noticed an aquarium that contained, among other species of fish, a seahorse. She watched this seahorse swim from one end of the tank to the other; continually banging its head along the glass. For a long time, she thought how her own life felt this way, unable to be released from the failure to make her marriage work. After quite some time, she walked to the tank, took the meshed scoop and lifted the seahorse out of the tank. She walked to the beach and released the seahorse to the ocean. She then realized that the only way she was going to help herself was to lift herself out of her own container and learn to live again.

The seahorse has become a constant reminder to me that we have choices in life. We can stay unsettled in situations or we can step away and revisit our lives. Accepting this has helped me to connect with the faith we have been given to make these choices. We may not always make the right choices, but if we step away and release ourselves, we will gain the capability to view what is best for us as we move forward.

You will notice depictions of seahorses on the following pages, marking possibilities of new beginnings. Just as the seahorse labored to escape, so we struggle in an attempt to allow our hearts and minds, through faith and choice, to determine our own destiny, perhaps by first forgiving ourselves.

Table of Contents

Stage One – Shades of Grief 11
Month One 11
Month Two 27
Month Three 42

Stage Two – Seeking Comfort 58
Month One 58
Month Two 74
Month Three 89

Stage Three – Deliberate Distractions 105
Month One 105
Month Two 121
Month Three 136

Stage Four – Honoring the Memory 152
Month One 152
Month Two 168
Month Three 183

How to Use Your Journal

Prompts have been designed to help you if you feel compelled to write something but are not sure "what to say."

The prompts have been mindfully written. In addition, somewhere along your journey, a quotation, a day, a moment, may touch you with a thought. Write it down.

Stage One

Shades of Grief

The initial waves of grief are very difficult. We find ourselves asking "Why Me? Why is this happening to me? Why is it happening now? How am I going to get through this?" The thoughts revolve around ourselves and how we ever are going to be able to cope. The highest waves come crashing on us, sweeping us emotionally and we feel lost at sea.

Month One

Day 1

Don't people know what to say to me when I am grieving?

_____

_____

_____

_____

_____

_____

Stage One - Shades of Grief

Month One ◆ Day 2

Anger hits me in different ways when I am least expecting it.

_____

_____

_____

_____

Month One ◆ Day 3

Why do people say things that aren't helpful?

_____

_____

_____

_____

Stage One – Shades of Grief

Month One ♦ Day 4

Seeing others holding hands can make me sad.

Month One ♦ Day 5

I hate it when people say I should be getting over this. Maybe I don't want to!

Stage One - Shades of Grief

Month One ◆ Day 6

Why can't I tell people exactly how I feel?

_____
_____
_____
_____

Month One ◆ Day 7

I find it annoying when people tell me "You need to get over this."

_____
_____
_____
_____
_____

Stage One - Shades of Grief

Month One ◆ Day 8

It hurts so much to think about him because I miss him so much.

Month One ◆ Day 9

My whole world has changed.

Stage One - Shades of Grief

Month One ◆ Day 10

Sometimes hearing others speak of their loss makes me feel worse.

_____

_____

_____

_____

Month One ◆ Day 11

I can't get past the anger I feel towards almost everyone.

_____

_____

_____

_____

Stage One - Shades of Grief

Month One ♦ Day 12

It is hard not to focus on "Why did this happen?"

___

Month One ♦ Day 13

I don't know if I can ever accept that things will never be the same.

Stage One - Shades of Grief

Month One ◆ Day 14

Sometimes well-intentioned people say all the wrong things.

_____

_____

_____

_____

Month One ◆ Day 15

Some days I don't want to "get over this."

_____

_____

_____

_____

_____

Stage One – Shades of Grief

Month One ◆ Day 16

I miss you when . . .

Month One ◆ Day 17

Pain itself will not change, only its intensity.

Stage One – Shades of Grief

Month One ◆ Day 18

Some days I just feel numb and cannot move.

_____

_____

_____

_____

Month One ◆ Day 19

How will I manage alone without her companionship?

_____

_____

_____

_____

Stage One - Shades of Grief

Month One ♦ Day 20

Right now nothing feels safe.

Month One ♦ Day 21

At the moment it happened I was changed and I will <u>never</u> be the same.

Stage One - Shades of Grief

Month One ◆ Day 22

I feel that a part of me has died and I wonder if I will ever heal.

_____

_____

_____

_____

Month One ◆ Day 23

There are so many questions and not enough answers.

_____

_____

_____

_____

Stage One – Shades of Grief

Month One ◆ Day 23

I am trying to remember that people mean well when they say things that are insensitive.

_____

_____

_____

_____

Month One ◆ Day 24

I feel most angry when . . .

_____

_____

_____

_____

Stage One – Shades of Grief

Month One ◆ Day 26

Not everyone understands that this experience changes everyone in different ways.

Month One ◆ Day 27

I want people to ask me how I am feeling—not how I am doing!

Stage One - Shades of Grief

Month One ◆ Day 28

When I am raw with grief, I do not want to hear, "Have a Nice Day!"

___

___

___

___

Month One ◆ Day 29

I need to tell myself that his leaving me was not meant to hurt me.

___

___

___

___

Stage One - Shades of Grief

Month One ♦ Day 30

I just can't make myself open the door to her clothes closet.

Stage One - Shades of Grief

Month Two ◆ Day 1

Why does everyone act like everything is okay when my world has fallen apart?

_____

_____

_____

_____

Month Two ◆ Day 2

When I look at other people who still have what I have lost, I feel jealous, angry, cheated, and abandoned.

_____

_____

_____

_____

Stage One – Shades of Grief

Month Two ◆ Day 3

I think of our life together and the good times, then am suddenly awakened by the harsh reality that I am alone.

_____

_____

_____

_____

Month Two ◆ Day 4

Anger can be frightening.

_____

_____

_____

_____

Stage One – Shades of Grief

Month Two ◆ Day 5

This journey is taking everything out of me; I have nothing else to give.

Month Two ◆ Day 6

I feel so lonely because I can't share my most private thoughts with her.

Stage One - Shades of Grief

Month Two ◆ Day 7

How can my friends seem to forget what I am going through?

_____

_____

_____

_____

Month Two ◆ Day 8

Sometimes crying in the shower helps release the pain.

_____

_____

_____

_____

Stage One – Shades of Grief

Month Two ◆ Day 9

I think I should be adjusting better, but I feel so alone.

Month Two ◆ Day 10

I am on an emotional roller coaster without a track; maybe I should seek help.

Stage One – Shades of Grief

Month Two ◆ Day 11

Sometimes I just feel stranded.

Month Two ◆ Day 12

I am going to try to talk to him when I feel lonely and awake at night.

Stage One – Shades of Grief

Month Two ♦ Day 13

I need to remind myself that what angers me can also control me.

___

Month Two ♦ Day 14

I feel closest to you when . . .

Stage One – Shades of Grief

Month Two ◆ Day 15

A place where I feel safe to cry is . . .

_____
_____
_____
_____

Month Two ◆ Day 16

There are times when I think no one can understand my constant sadness.

_____
_____
_____
_____

Stage One – Shades of Grief

Month Two ◆ Day 17

I sometimes feel lonely even in a crowd of people.

_____

_____

_____

_____

Month Two ◆ Day 18

I know we enter and leave this world alone, but I've never lived completely alone before.

_____

_____

_____

_____

_____

Stage One – Shades of Grief

Month Two ◆ Day 19

I should write down the kind and helpful things people say to me.

_____

_____

_____

_____

Month Two ◆ Day 20

Will I ever fill the emptiness I feel?

_____

_____

_____

_____

Stage One – Shades of Grief

Month Two ◆ Day 21

This loss is a painful lesson to learn.

___

Month Two ◆ Day 22

When I look at greeting cards, I need to understand it is okay to laugh and cry at the same time.

Stage One - Shades of Grief

Month Two ◆ Day 23

I can't bear to think I will never see her again.

_____

_____

_____

_____

Month Two ◆ Day 24

I am trying to remember . . .

_____

_____

_____

_____

_____

Stage One - Shades of Grief

Month Two ◆ Day 25

I feel fearful without being able to describe it.

Month Two ◆ Day 26

Sometimes I start to laugh when I think of something funny she did; then I cry because I miss her so much.

Stage One – Shades of Grief

Month Two ♦ Day 27

Thinking about my childhood and old friends helps me forget my sadness for a little while.

___

Month Two ♦ Day 28

I should try to see what has helped others to see if it can help me as well.

Stage One - Shades of Grief

Month Two ◆ Day 29

If I can't sleep and I feel like crying, then I should cry.

Month Two ◆ Day 30

I am trying to realize that my loss can sometimes weaken even someone as strong as I am.

Stage One - Shades of Grief

Month Three ◆ Day 1

I hurt so much it is hard to even remember, let alone be thankful for, the good times we had.

___

Month Three ◆ Day 2

If you were here, I would tell you . . .

___

Stage One - Shades of Grief

Month Three ◆ Day 3

If I go to a public place and watch people, maybe I will realize others are also dealing with difficulties.

Month Three ◆ Day 4

I would go to church but the hymns make me cry.

Stage One - Shades of Grief

Month Three ♦ Day 5

I am afraid to return to my favorite pastime because it makes me sad.

___

Month Three ♦ Day 6

Memories and words can arouse mixed feelings. I can think of several right now.

Stage One - Shades of Grief

Month Three ◆ Day 7

The movie "My Life" makes me cry and laugh.

_____

_____

_____

_____

Month Three ◆ Day 8

Why do I feel most alone when I am in a crowd?

_____

_____

_____

_____

Stage One – Shades of Grief

Month Three ◆ Day 9

Sometimes I feel like I am building a fence around myself.

_____

_____

_____

_____

Month Three ◆ Day 10

I need to select what is helpful and what is not from what others say to me.

_____

_____

_____

_____

Stage One - Shades of Grief

Month Three ♦ Day 11

I need to be comforted, but my anger holds me back.

Month Three ♦ Day 12

I sometimes question my faith, endlessly asking "Why?"

Stage One – Shades of Grief

Month Three ◆ Day 13

I need to to talk to others who can share my loss.

_____

_____

_____

_____

Month Three ◆ Day 14

Finding hope is not easy, but it is doable.

_____

_____

_____

_____

Stage One - Shades of Grief

Month Three ◆ Day 15

I often think about how things could have been different.

Month Three ◆ Day 16

I didn't realize how much this loss would bring back the memory of other losses.

Stage One - Shades of Grief

Month Three ♦ Day 17

I need to be aware of what is going on in my own heart, not dwelling on what others may have experienced.

_____

_____

_____

_____

Month Three ♦ Day 18

Sometimes I feel angry, frustrated, and sad all at the same time.

_____

_____

_____

_____

Stage One – Shades of Grief

Month Three ◆ Day 19

It is okay for me to talk out loud about my hurt, even if no one is listening.

_____

_____

_____

_____

Month Three ◆ Day 20

I am learning that my pain can take a different approach every day.

_____

_____

_____

_____

Stage One – Shades of Grief

Month Three ◆ Day 21

I can't help but ask "Why me?"

_____

_____

_____

_____

Month Three ◆ Day 22

I wish he were here to fix things. Whom do I call? Where do I start?

_____

_____

_____

_____

_____

Stage One – Shades of Grief

Month Three ♦ Day 23

What do I do with this poor, sad person I see in the mirror?

_____

_____

_____

_____

Month Three ♦ Day 24

Sometimes I simply want to scream!

_____

_____

_____

_____

Stage One – Shades of Grief

Month Three ◆ Day 25

Some days I have to ask myself, "Why bother?"

_____

_____

_____

_____

Month Three ◆ Day 26

This just isn't fair.

_____

_____

_____

_____

Stage One – Shades of Grief

Month Three ♦ Day 27

This all seems like a bad dream. When will I wake up?

Month Three ♦ Day 28

I have never felt so afraid of life before.

Stage One – Shades of Grief

Month Three ◆ Day 29

Sometimes I am sure I am losing my grip on reality.

_____

_____

_____

_____

Month Three ◆ Day 30

I am afraid and angry about everything. There seems to be no hope.

_____

_____

_____

_____

_____

Stage Two

Seeking Comfort

The second phase of grief may initially seem to be smooth because we need to be focused on the forms and minutiae of details required of us at this time. However, dealing with difficult telephone calls or letters can be a point at which reality hits. We often don't realize that deep, searing grief still awaits us. Even though we may be coping outwardly and others may surmise that we "are doing well," in reality we are likely to be experiencing a roller coaster of emotions, physical changes, behavior, and spiritual questions.

Month One

Day 1

I can now give myself permission to grieve because I am allowed to feel this.

Stage Two - Seeking Comfort

Month One ♦ Day 2

I am looking from a totally different perspective now, and what was important before no longer is.

Month One ♦ Day 3

Sometimes I can sense her presence when I most need to feel it and sometimes when I least expect it.

Stage Two – Seeking Comfort

Month One ♦ Day 4

Much of what mattered before seems trivial now.

_____

_____

_____

_____

Month One ♦ Day 5

When people speak to me I will try to listen with my ears rather than my eyes.

_____

_____

_____

_____

Stage Two – Seeking Comfort

Month One ♦ Day 6

I yearn for his touch.

Month One ♦ Day 7

Sometimes I think that if I could schedule the time to grieve, I could handle it better.

Stage Two – Seeking Comfort

Month One ◆ Day 8

I often think of happier times, but remain saddened by the confusion and frustration this loss has left for me.

___

Month One ◆ Day 9

I miss being in the same house with her.

Stage Two - Seeking Comfort

Month One ♦ Day 10

We can plan our lives; we cannot plan for grief.

Month One ♦ Day 11

I ask myself, "Who are you now?" My role and identity may no longer be what it was as a spouse, friend, sister, brother, son, daughter, or parent.

Stage Two – Seeking Comfort

Month One ♦ Day 12

Confusion can result in days passing by me without my realizing it. How can I get back on track?

_____

_____

_____

_____

Month One ♦ Day 13

I ache to see his smile.

_____

_____

_____

_____

Stage Two – Seeking Comfort

Month One ◆ Day 14

Dreary days may bring dreary thoughts and I need to view this as part of the healing.

Month One ◆ Day 15

I miss her to the point of tears.

Stage Two - Seeking Comfort

Month One ◆ Day 16

The labor of grieving and healing is different for everyone.

_____
_____
_____
_____

Month One ◆ Day 17

It is difficult to function when my thoughts are going in so many directions.

_____
_____
_____
_____
_____

Stage Two – Seeking Comfort

Month One ◆ Day 18

There is so much more I want to tell him and I suddenly realize there always will be things I'll want to share.

Month One ◆ Day 19

I used to accept that my feelings of grief may be heightened when I am not feeling physically well.

Stage Two – Seeking Comfort

Month One ♦ Day 20

While I have much to be thankful for, it is difficult when I miss her so much.

___

Month One ♦ Day 21

I just went to a place we both loved and visualized his presence at this place.

Stage Two - Seeking Comfort

Month One ♦ Day 22

Crying can release the sadness of grief. I can take the time I need for this.

Month One ♦ Day 23

Today my heart is saying one thing and my head is saying something different.

Stage Two - Seeking Comfort

Month One ◆ Day 24

I sometimes feel lonely in a crowd of people because I am used to having her with me.

Month One ◆ Day 25

I do not need to set aside grieving because I am spending time on paperwork and packing precious belongings; sometimes tasks and grieving work together.

Stage Two - Seeking Comfort

Month One ♦ Day 26

Today I found myself gazing at something for a long time without knowing what I was looking for.

Month One ♦ Day 27

Sometimes I walk by someone wearing her perfume or his cologne. I take in the scent and smile in remembrance.

Stage Two – Seeking Comfort

Month One ◆ Day 28

I wish my life could be put on hold for a while so I would have time to think and mourn without interruption.

_____
_____
_____
_____

Month One ◆ Day 29

What can I say when someone wants to help and my mind is a blank?

_____
_____
_____
_____
_____

Stage Two - Seeking Comfort

Month One ♦ Day 30

It can be comforting to think the one I love and miss is watching over me.

Stage Two - Seeking Comfort

Month Two ◆ Day 1

Grief is emotion; mourning is the expression of that emotion.

_____
_____
_____
_____

Month Two ◆ Day 2

When I look into the mirror, I am not sure whom I see anymore.

_____
_____
_____
_____
_____

Stage Two – Seeking Comfort

Month Two ◆ Day 3

Shopping for cards can be difficult when I find myself reading one that is speaking personally to my own feelings.

_____

_____

_____

_____

Month Two ◆ Day 4

Grieving can be private or shared—or both.

_____

_____

_____

_____

Stage Two - Seeking Comfort

Month Two ◆ Day 5

Words don't always fit the way I am feeling.

Month Two ◆ Day 6

I may wear a piece of clothing or jewelry that was hers and feel it touching me throughout the day and night.

Stage Two – Seeking Comfort

Month Two ◆ Day 7

In grief sometimes a heart aches just because it has to.

_____

_____

_____

_____

Month Two ◆ Day 8

Why am I happy and sad at the same time?

_____

_____

_____

_____

_____

Stage Two - Seeking Comfort

Month Two ◆ Day 9

Some people ask for a sign that a loved one is fine. I like to just close my eyes and think about her or what she so loved.

_____

_____

_____

_____

Month Two ◆ Day 10

Grieving can make me feel totally empty inside.

_____

_____

_____

_____

Stage Two - Seeking Comfort

Month Two ◆ Day 11

I planned my life, but was not prepared for this loss.

_____

_____

_____

_____

Month Two ◆ Day 12

I am trying not to avoid talking to him.

_____

_____

_____

_____

Stage Two - Seeking Comfort

Month Two ◆ Day 13

Grief can feel like an explosion just happened in or around me.

_____

_____

_____

_____

Month Two ◆ Day 14

Sometimes I feel as though I am just going through the motions of living.

_____

_____

_____

_____

Stage Two – Seeking Comfort

Month Two ◆ Day 15

If I cry, that's okay; friends understand.

Month Two ◆ Day 16

I must grieve my own way and not worry about what others think.

Stage Two - Seeking Comfort

Month Two ◆ Day 17

Sometimes I feel helpless to get anything accomplished.

Month Two ◆ Day 18

Feeling and embracing her presence can give me comfort.

Stage Two – Seeking Comfort

Month Two ◆ Day 19

Grief can't be scheduled. I will let it happen as it happens.

_____

_____

_____

_____

Month Two ◆ Day 20

I feel anxiety, not knowing which direction my life is going.

_____

_____

_____

_____

Stage Two - Seeking Comfort

Month Two ◆ Day 21

Sometimes I close my eyes and think about his smile.

_____

_____

_____

_____

Month Two ◆ Day 22

Often the deepest grieving begins several months after the loss of a loved one.

_____

_____

_____

_____

Stage Two – Seeking Comfort

Month Two ◆ Day 23

I wish we had had more time together before I lost him.

Month Two ◆ Day 24

I like watching the birds, noticing a particular one and letting it represent my loved one, showing me she is okay.

Stage Two - Seeking Comfort

Month Two ◆ Day 25

I sometimes can feel grief taking over my body physically, even to the point of feeling cold or numb.

_____

_____

_____

_____

Month Two ◆ Day 26

At times I find it impossible to accept that someone I loved is gone.

_____

_____

_____

_____

Stage Two – Seeking Comfort

Month Two ◆ Day 27

I remember how my mother enjoyed watching "her" birds, and I think she would communicate with me in this way.

_____

_____

_____

_____

Month Two ◆ Day 28

I believe that a person can never grieve too much.

_____

_____

_____

_____

Stage Two - Seeking Comfort

Month Two ◆ Day 29

The feeling of loss can strike at any time; how can I be prepared?

_____

_____

_____

_____

_____

Month Two ◆ Day 30

I think I shall ask for a sign from him and see what thoughts may come to my mind through him.

_____

_____

_____

_____

_____

Stage Two - Seeking Comfort

Month Three ♦ Day 1

Grief can feel like my heart has been ripped from my body and that I will never be whole again.

___

Month Three ♦ Day 2

I find myself reliving the loss again and again and asking "What if?"

Stage Two - Seeking Comfort

Month Three ◆ Day 3

He always called me when he saw the first robin in the spring. I will watch for the first robin.

Month Three ◆ Day 4

She loved red cardinals, so I will find comfort watching them.

Stage Two – Seeking Comfort

Month Three ◆ Day 5

No one can tell me that it will get better. It will not. Rather, as time passes, I will learn to live with my grief.

Month Three ◆ Day 6

While I understand that life ends, I still ask myself, "Why now?"

Stage Two – Seeking Comfort

Month Three ◆ Day 7

I will not hide my tears; I will see this as sensing the presence of the one I continue to love.

___

___

___

___

Month Three ◆ Day 8

I need to remember that right now I have the right to be happy or sad at any given moment.

___

___

___

___

Stage Two - Seeking Comfort

Month Three ◆ Day 9

I will visit his aunt, mother or sister to share information about him that one of us might not have known.

_____

_____

_____

_____

Month Three ◆ Day 10

When I particularly need to feel her presence, I will go to a place she loved, perhap her favorite park.

_____

_____

_____

_____

Stage Two - Seeking Comfort

Month Three ◆ Day 11

It is okay to ask for a hug if I need one.

___

Month Three ◆ Day 12

I will find a quiet place and listen to my favorite music.

Stage Two - Seeking Comfort

Month Three ◆ Day 13

The next time I see a butterfly, I will think of her because she always made me smile.

___

Month Three ◆ Day 14

I used to enjoy the warmth of the sun; maybe I still can.

Stage Two - Seeking Comfort

Month Three ◆ Day 15

I am trying to remember the numbness that allows us to handle initial moments of loss.

_____

_____

_____

_____

Month Three ◆ Day 16

I will go for a long drive and talk aloud to myself.

_____

_____

_____

_____

Stage Two – Seeking Comfort

Month Three ◆ Day 17

The day may be beautiful, but sometimes the emptiness is overwhelming.

_____

_____

_____

_____

Month Three ◆ Day 18

I will always see something in someone else that reminds me of him.

_____

_____

_____

_____

_____

Stage Two - Seeking Comfort

Month Three ♦ Day 19

It is difficult not to let my sadness bring me down.

___

___

___

___

Month Three ♦ Day 20

I need to look forward, difficult as it is.

___

___

___

___

Stage Two – Seeking Comfort

Month Three ◆ Day 21

When I feel fragile, I will seek someone who can be gentle.

Month Three ◆ Day 22

If I would make a drawing of a pie and label each slice with the name of a task into which I place my energy, I need to allocate at least one slice for me to be myself.

Stage Two - Seeking Comfort

Month Three ◆ Day 23

It helps to breathe deeply before I approach a task that is difficult for me to face.

Month Three ◆ Day 24

When I am alone, I will try to relax by singing or dancing to music.

Stage Two – Seeking Comfort

Month Three ◆ Day 25

When I feel weary, I will take the time to rest to rejuvenate myself so I can keep going forward.

Month Three ◆ Day 26

Even if I can accomplish only a few things, I can feel productive.

Stage Two - Seeking Comfort

Month Three ◆ Day 27

I believe that the intensity of my pain is a reflection of just how much I loved him.

_____

_____

_____

_____

Month Three ◆ Day 28

When I see a crowd, I wonder how many of the people are also hurting from a loss.

_____

_____

_____

_____

Stage Two – Seeking Comfort

Month Three ♦ Day 29

I experience so many emotions that I find it difficult to describe them.

Month Three ♦ Day 30

When I think of her, I return to a place where she was happy.

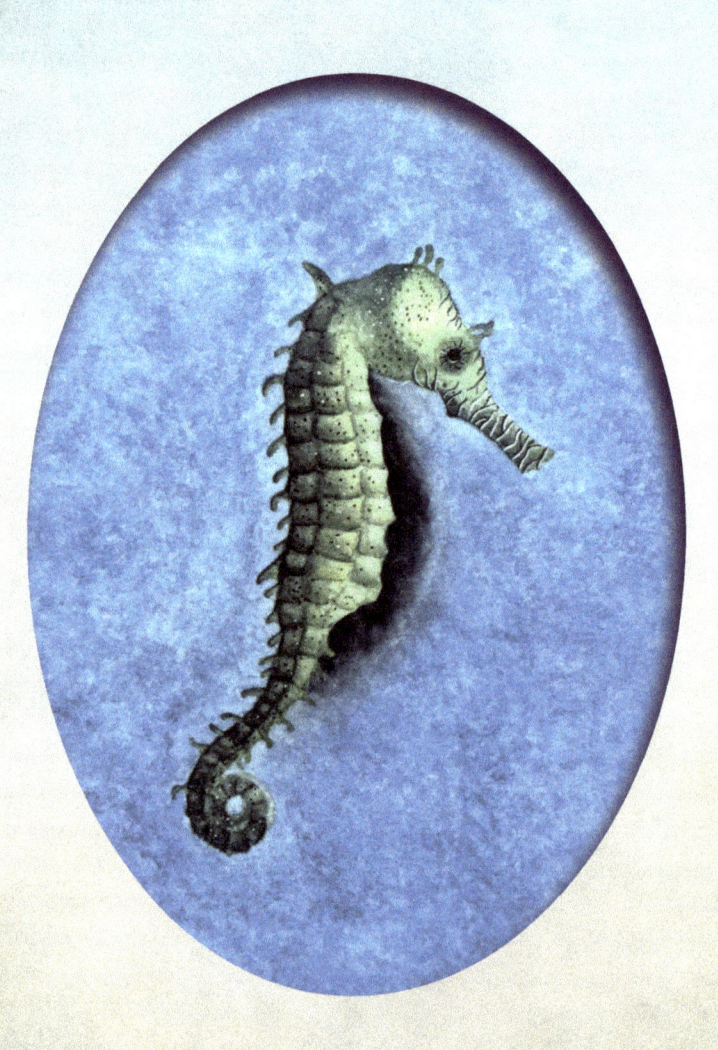

Stage Three

Deliberate Distractions

We ask ourselves, "How do I incorporate all these changes in my world? Am I doing it correctly? What is right for me to be doing now? Did I do my best to show my love?" Emotions are changing during this time and our priorities take on a different perspective. We need to remember to re-determine our purpose in our new world. Often we begin to feel more compassion for others.

Month One

Day 1

I treasure those who support me through this journey.

_____

_____

_____

_____

_____

_____

Stage Three - Deliberate Distractions

Month One ◆ Day 2

Seeing the snowfall as the gray clouds roll by can be comforting.

_____

_____

_____

_____

Month One ◆ Day 3

If she were here today, she would share my feelings in silence with me.

_____

_____

_____

_____

Stage Three – Deliberate Distractions

Month One ◆ Day 4

Sometimes I remember what a significant impact he made on my life and I hope I did the same for him.

___

Month One ◆ Day 5

It helps me to share my story and I am grateful for those who listen.

Stage Three – Deliberate Distractions

Month One ◆ Day 6

When sorrow strikes it sometimes is difficult to see beauty, but I can try to enjoy the autumn leaves, blue skies, and snow-covered mountains.

_____
_____
_____
_____

Month One ◆ Day 7

Sometimes I need someone to just listen, not feeling it necessary to respond.

_____
_____
_____
_____

Stage Three – Deliberate Distractions

Month One ◆ Day 8

I wonder if she truly knew how much I loved her.

Month One ◆ Day 9

I will try to listen attentively to the stories and sorrows of others to realize we all live through these experiences.

Stage Three – Deliberate Distractions

Month One ◆ Day 10

If I find myself wondering where everyone went now that I need them the most, I will remind myself to call someone who has offered to help.

_____

_____

_____

_____

Month One ◆ Day 11

I may have to take the lead and ask for help from those who want to help and may not know how.

_____

_____

_____

_____

Stage Three – Deliberate Distractions

Month One ♦ Day 12

This may be a good day to begin to organize scrapbooks and photograph albums for the times we shared.

Month One ♦ Day 13

This might be a good time to begin tracking the moon to its fullness for several months.

Stage Three – Deliberate Distractions

Month One ◆ Day 14

I also need those who I know will just be there for me, supportive, not judging.

_____

_____

_____

_____

Month One ◆ Day 15

I will buy a tree or flowering shrubs and plant them at the right time and in a place where I can watch them grow.

_____

_____

_____

_____

Stage Three - Deliberate Distractions

Month One ♦ Day 16

My memory will keep him alive in my heart and soul.

_____

_____

_____

_____

Month One ♦ Day 17

I realize that not everyone is comfortable with a hug.

_____

_____

_____

_____

_____

Stage Three – Deliberate Distractions

Month One ◆ Day 18

Today I will take a walk and be very observant of what is around me.

_____

_____

_____

_____

Month One ◆ Day 19

This is what I would like to say to him about my enduring love for him.

_____

_____

_____

_____

Stage Three – Deliberate Distractions

Month One ♦ Day 20

If I don't want to be hugged, I will say so.

___

Month One ♦ Day 21

I am going to visit a spot where I can enjoy the beauty of our world.

Stage Three – Deliberate Distractions

Month One ◆ Day 22

I am learning to treasure each moment of remembrance and not assume the same moment will be there again.

_____

_____

_____

_____

Month One ◆ Day 23

How am I supposed to deal with all of the reminders of our love?

_____

_____

_____

_____

Stage Three – Deliberate Distractions

Month One ◆ Day 24

When friends offer to help me, I will give them something to do.

_____

_____

_____

_____

Month One ◆ Day 25

I feel like running away from all of this hurt, but I know when I return, the feelings will still be there.

_____

_____

_____

_____

Stage Three – Deliberate Distractions

Month One ◆ Day 26

How can I be sure she knew how I felt? Will I always be in her heart?

_____

_____

_____

_____

Month One ◆ Day 27

I am thinking of how I felt when someone remembered me with a gift. Maybe it is time to return that kindness.

_____

_____

_____

_____

Stage Three - Deliberate Distractions

Month One ◆ Day 28

Knowing I provided unconditional love can make me smile throughout the day.

Month One ◆ Day 29

Knowing the deep love we shared helps me feel the love still with me.

Stage Three – Deliberate Distractions

Month One ♦ Day 30

While my teddy bear is no substitute, holding it comforts me while I think of how much I loved him.

Stage Three - Deliberate Distractions

Month Two ◆ Day 1

I feel her presence when I see something that reminds me of her.

___

Month Two ◆ Day 2

Some days not even the warm sun can help the coolness of my broken heart.

Stage Three - Deliberate Distractions

Month Two ◆ Day 3

I will make a list and find a worthy cause for which I might volunteer to help.

_____
_____
_____
_____

Month Two ◆ Day 4

I think I will write her a letter to tell her how I feel; I'll put it in an envelope and read it again later.

_____
_____
_____
_____

Stage Three - Deliberate Distractions

Month Two ◆ Day 5

I need to remind myself not to say I am doing fine if I am not.

Month Two ◆ Day 6

It is okay to speak aloud what I need to say to her.

Stage Three – Deliberate Distractions

Month Two ♦ Day 7

What is something that once made me laugh?

_____

_____

_____

_____

Month Two ♦ Day 8

I relied on her more than I ever realized.

_____

_____

_____

_____

Stage Three - Deliberate Distractions

Month Two ♦ Day 9

I had almost forgotten how comforting to both body and thought a hot bath can be.

_____

_____

_____

_____

Month Two ♦ Day 10

I will thank those who understand what I am going through.

_____

_____

_____

_____

Stage Three – Deliberate Distractions

Month Two ◆ Day 11

Not only will I miss him personally, but also I will miss what I'll never have again with him.

___

___

___

___

Month Two ◆ Day 12

I will plan a trip alone for a couple of days and take a few comforting items with me.

___

___

___

___

Stage Three – Deliberate Distractions

Month Two ♦ Day 13

I need to remember that she loved me and still does, but in a different way and place.

Month Two ♦ Day 14

I remember how I treasure silence in a quiet place.

Stage Three – Deliberate Distractions

Month Two ◆ Day 15

Today I really need him—and miss him beyond words.

_____

_____

_____

_____

Month Two ◆ Day 16

While people tell me to stay busy, I sometimes prefer solitude.

_____

_____

_____

_____

Stage Three - Deliberate Distractions

Month Two ◆ Day 17

Maybe this evening I will watch a humorous movie. It might help to laugh again.

_____

_____

_____

_____

Month Two ◆ Day 18

Walking is a wonderful way to allow my thoughts to reflect feelings which may then turn into action.

_____

_____

_____

_____

_____

Stage Three – Deliberate Distractions

Month Two ◆ Day 19

I may sleep under the stars one night to understand that life goes on.

Month Two ◆ Day 20

My appreciation for him continues even though he isn't here.

Stage Three – Deliberate Distractions

Month Two ♦ Day 21

As I watch the clouds form various shapes, I will let my mind wander.

___

Month Two ♦ Day 22

I will love him forever.

Stage Three - Deliberate Distractions

Month Two ◆ Day 23

I know I cannot continue to look back at what I could have done or not done.

_____

_____

_____

_____

Month Two ◆ Day 24

I expect that sometimes I'll laugh when I think of a funny story about us. Then I will probably cry.

_____

_____

_____

_____

Stage Three – Deliberate Distractions

Month Two ♦ Day 25

Sometimes it is just the simple companionship of someone who cared about me that I most miss.

_____

_____

_____

_____

Month Two ♦ Day 26

I should begin to search for new meaning in my life, perhaps based on what my loved one meant to me.

_____

_____

_____

_____

Stage Three - Deliberate Distractions

Month Two ◆ Day 27

I should take this weekend simply to reflect on a thought or feeling.

Month Two ◆ Day 28

When I pick up the phone to call him, the harsh reality sets in and, again, I realize just how much I miss him.

Stage Three – Deliberate Distractions

Month Two ◆ Day 29

If I am ready to be distracted a little, I will invite a friend to go with me for coffee.

___

Month Two ◆ Day 30

I know the love of my life will be in my heart forever. I will cherish the memories.

Stage Three – Deliberate Distractions

Month Three • Day 1

I had not realized before my loss that missing someone so much does not always allow a person to think clearly.

_____

_____

_____

_____

Month Three • Day 2

Looking back over the many holiday seasons and family get-togethers, I find myself wondering what the next one will be like without him.

_____

_____

_____

_____

Stage Three – Deliberate Distractions

Month Three ◆ Day 3

The stars—shining brightly and ever present—always remind me of the one I have lost.

Month Three ◆ Day 4

Exercise can give me some personal quiet time with both my physical and emotional selves.

Stage Three - Deliberate Distractions

Month Three ◆ Day 5

I shall go to the beach, lake, or river and think about how I am going to take care of me.

_____

_____

_____

_____

Month Three ◆ Day 6

Today I will call a friend who also lost a loved one, even though it has not been recently.

_____

_____

_____

_____

Stage Three – Deliberate Distractions

Month Three ♦ Day 7

Perhaps a massage would help me relax.

Month Three ♦ Day 8

I want to see if a chocolate milkshake or cup of hot chocolate still can be delicious and soothing.

Stage Three - Deliberate Distractions

Month Three ♦ Day 9

I think I am ready to once again awaken in the morning to my favorite music and then go for a long walk.

Month Three ♦ Day 10

What will next year be like—and the year after that? I wonder if I will miss her as much—knowing that I will.

Stage Three - Deliberate Distractions

Month Three ♦ Day 11

I am going to visit a spot where I can enjoy the beauty of our world.

Month Three ♦ Day 12

I will research local support groups to find one that may be a good fit for me, even if I decide I don't want to join.

Stage Three – Deliberate Distractions

Month Three ◆ Day 13

If I join a support group, I will attend for three weeks and if I am not comfortable with it, I will leave.

Month Three ◆ Day 14

I will make myself attend a social event, but will drive myself just in case I feel the need to go home.

Stage Three - Deliberate Distractions

Month Three ◆ Day 15

I will accept with gratitude compassion from all.

___

Month Three ◆ Day 16

Today I will remember her and smile.

Stage Three – Deliberate Distractions

Month Three ♦ Day 17

The fresh morning air serves as a reminder to take care of myself.

_____

_____

_____

_____

Month Three ♦ Day 18

I will think about writing my thoughts in the form of letters or this journal; I believe I will be glad to have saved these when I read them later.

_____

_____

_____

_____

Stage Three – Deliberate Distractions

Month Three ◆ Day 19

All I need to do is think of his smile and I start smiling in spite of my sorrow.

Month Three ◆ Day 20

I will remind myself every day to think of the blessings in my life just by knowing her.

Stage Three - Deliberate Distractions

Month Three ◆ Day 21

Going through my own grief has put me more in touch with the losses of others.

_____

_____

_____

_____

Month Three ◆ Day 22

I am working on accepting what I can't change.

_____

_____

_____

_____

Stage Three - Deliberate Distractions

Month Three ◆ Day 23

Moving forward is all I can do, though I yearn for what is no longer.

_____

_____

_____

_____

Month Three ◆ Day 24

Every time the phone rings, I am still sometimes hopeful that this bad dream is over.

_____

_____

_____

_____

Stage Three - Deliberate Distractions

Month Three ◆ Day 25

Seasons of change, security, identity—I need to restructure who I am and how I now fit in my world.

___

___

___

___

Month Three ◆ Day 26

If we could have just one hour together . . .

___

___

___

___

___

Stage Three – Deliberate Distractions

Month Three ◆ Day 27

Tomorrow I will try to . . .

___

___

___

___

Month Three ◆ Day 28

I still find it difficult to . . .

___

___

___

___

Stage Three - Deliberate Distractions

Month Three ♦ Day 29

I regret not saying . . .

_____

_____

_____

_____

Month Three ♦ Day 30

My mind says I need to move forward, but my heart is having a hard time.

_____

_____

_____

_____

Stage Four

Honoring the Memory

Coming to terms with various possibilities is usually our final stage. Confusion and frustration are replaced with less bewilderment. The waves of hurt, anger, loss, and uncertainty still ebb and flow without our knowing when this will end. Finally, the waves become incorporated into our world and we are ready for the next juncture. We realize that, while the grief remains part of us, we do find ourselves again and can honor the one we have lost.

Month One
Day 1

As I near the first year anniversary of my loss, I will try to think of it as closing out a painful year.

_____
_____
_____
_____
_____
_____
_____

Stage Four - Honoring the Memory

Month One ◆ Day 2

I will seek what a new year brings in unexpected joy and be ready to deal with any unanticipated pain.

___

Month One ◆ Day 3

I believe I am ready to seek an activity, hobby, or commitment for which I can become impassioned.

Stage Four – Honoring the Memory

Month One ◆ Day 4

Coping strategies are often different for each person and for each loss. I am beginning to find the ones right for me.

_____

_____

_____

_____

Month One ◆ Day 5

Now may be the time to develop a new skill.

_____

_____

_____

_____

Stage Four – Honoring the Memory

Month One ◆ Day 6

Some days I consider the time ahead that I might feel love again.

Month One ◆ Day 7

I still have gifts of myself to give and while the gift of love I had cannot be replaced, I can perhaps re-direct it.

Stage Four - Honoring the Memory

Month One ◆ Day 8

I will try to treasure all transitions, for I understand we cannot go through life without them.

___

___

___

___

Month One ◆ Day 9

I am beginning to feel assured that I did the best I could for her and I am content.

___

___

___

___

Stage Four – Honoring the Memory

Month One ♦ Day 10

Each of us is given more opportunities in life than we could ever have imagined. I am preparing now to accept new ones.

Month One ♦ Day 11

Even in grief we are given choices; I understand now that we need these choices to grow through our grief.

Stage Four – Honoring the Memory

Month One ◆ Day 12

It is difficult but I am learning to say good-bye, and I will never forget the life we shared.

Month One ◆ Day 13

Because this experience has changed me, I can view others' experiences with more empathy.

Stage Four – Honoring the Memory

Month One ◆ Day 14

We learn many lessons through this experience, one of which is forgiving as well as accepting forgiveness.

Month One ◆ Day 15

Saying good-bye to one we have loved reflects our belief that she will find peace during her journey and implies we will see her again.

Stage Four – Honoring the Memory

Month One ◆ Day 16

The time after the loss of a loved one goes so quickly that I can't keep track of where it went.

___

Month One ◆ Day 17

I am ready to seek new potentials and think about what I might have wanted to do but haven't. Perhaps his spirit will guide me.

Stage Four – Honoring the Memory

Month One ◆ Day 18

I will not avoid attending funeral services for friends, remembering how important their support was to me.

Month One ◆ Day 19

I will never again say to a newly bereaved person, "I know exactly how you feel."

Stage Four – Honoring the Memory

Month One ◆ Day 20

I may consider adopting a pet, for while this is a commitment, it is one of returned unconditional love.

Month One ◆ Day 21

I am trying to become accustomed to the new identity I now have.

Stage Four – Honoring the Memory

Month One ♦ Day 22

There are still moments when the feeling of emptiness is overwhelming. But now I recognize it for what it is and I have thought of things I can do that can be motivating.

___

Month One ♦ Day 23

I need to think if I can ever again accept loving, knowing it means taking a risk. Right now this is still frightening.

Stage Four – Honoring the Memory

Month One ◆ Day 24

When I see others living with pain in their hearts, I will offer a sincere word or gesture.

_____

_____

_____

_____

Month One ◆ Day 25

Through my own experience I have learned what to say to others who experience loss. I will use this skill.

_____

_____

_____

_____

Stage Four - Honoring the Memory

Month One ♦ Day 26

When a friend or acquaintance suffers a loss, I will reach out as one who understands.

_____

_____

_____

_____

Month One ♦ Day 27

When a best friend is marking the anniversary of a special date, I will call her, if only to leave a message.

_____

_____

_____

_____

Stage Four - Honoring the Memory

Month One ◆ Day 28

It is time to send a thank you note to those who have treated me with kindness.

___

Month One ◆ Day 29

I now look at the world from a different perspective. What once was important is no longer a priority.

Stage Four – Honoring the Memory

Month One ♦ Day 30

Elizabeth Kubler-Ross wrote, "People are like stained glass windows; they sparkle and shine when the sun is out, but when the darkness sets in, their true beauty is revealed only if there is a light within." I will strive to keep a light burning within my heart.

Stage Four – Honoring the Memory

Month Two ◆ Day 1

When a friend comes to visit, I may give that friend a small gift of thanks, perhaps something I have prepared.

_____

_____

_____

_____

Month Two ◆ Day 2

I will take something home baked to thank my co-workers for their support.

_____

_____

_____

_____

Stage Four – Honoring the Memory

Month Two ♦ Day 3

I may try to sleep with a pillow close to my side.

Month Two ♦ Day 4

I will find books that may comfort me.

Stage Four – Honoring the Memory

Month Two ◆ Day 5

I will take time to comfort others, just as they comforted me.

_____

_____

_____

_____

Month Two ◆ Day 6

I will take time to comfort myself, just as I comforted others.

_____

_____

_____

_____

Stage Four – Honoring the Memory

Month Two ♦ Day 7

Sometimes the motion of a rocking chair aids in reflection.

___

Month Two ♦ Day 8

When I feel the need for a warm embrace, it is okay to ask.

Stage Four – Honoring the Memory

Month Two ◆ Day 9

I need to remind myself that if I could choose the burdens or problems of someone else instead of my own, I likely would choose to keep my own.

Month Two ◆ Day 10

Despite all, I still need to take care of myself.

Stage Four – Honoring the Memory

Month Two ◆ Day 11

Even when there are moments when I feel overwhelmed, I now know I must continue to function.

Month Two ◆ Day 12

I am learning that when a day feels like it might be a good day, I need to treasure it.

Stage Four – Honoring the Memory

Month Two ◆ Day 13

I accept that when I feel like it, I can do something just for me.

___

Month Two ◆ Day 14

I try to listen to what my body tells me since I have learned that grief can affect me physically.

___

Stage Four – Honoring the Memory

Month Two ◆ Day 15

I will take some time to do nothing but listen to or think about something peaceful.

___

Month Two ◆ Day 16

Once in a while I will ask myself what I can do just for myself.

Stage Four – Honoring the Memory

Month Two ◆ Day 17

A physical wound changes many colors before it is healed; so will my feelings.

_____

_____

_____

_____

Month Two ◆ Day 18

I must be careful not to compare my journey to another's progress.

_____

_____

_____

_____

_____

Stage Four – Honoring the Memory

Month Two ◆ Day 19

I can keep busy for only so long; I need to stop before I become exhausted.

Month Two ◆ Day 20

I will be careful with mood-altering medications. They only mask what naturally needs to happen.

Stage Four – Honoring the Memory

Month Two ◆ Day 21

I should visit someone I have not seen in a long time.

_____

_____

_____

_____

Month Two ◆ Day 22

I will add love to everything I do.

_____

_____

_____

_____

Stage Four – Honoring the Memory

Month Two ◆ Day 23

While I see other problems, I realize I can cope only with what I now am dealing with.

___

Month Two ◆ Day 24

To be true to myself I will not hide or pretend this did not happen.

Stage Four – Honoring the Memory

Month Two ♦ Day 25

I need to think about how I have changed behaviorally, emotionally, physically, mentally, spiritually, and cognitively.

_____

_____

_____

_____

Month Two ♦ Day 26

I'll try not to question my actions, because I am adjusting to a new identity and that takes time.

_____

_____

_____

_____

Stage Four – Honoring the Memory

Month Two ◆ Day 27

Friends may not realize that what I am experiencing will change me.

___

Month Two ◆ Day 28

Today my goal is simply to function.

Stage Four – Honoring the Memory

Month Two ◆ Day 29

I will view the next adjustment as a possible new opportunity.

_____

_____

_____

_____

Month Two ◆ Day 30

I need to protect my energy level because I sometimes have too little of it.

_____

_____

_____

_____

Stage Four – Honoring the Memory

Month Three ◆ Day 1

I will share some stories of my loss with close friends, but will choose the words carefully.

_____

_____
_____

_____
_____

_____

Month Three ◆ Day 2

The impact others make in our lives is astounding; I will take time to remember them.

_____

_____

_____

_____

Stage Four – Honoring the Memory

Month Three ◆ Day 3

Having a beautiful day every now and then allows me to appreciate the gifts I have been given, including the opportunity to love even though I have lost someone.

Month Three ◆ Day 4

I will remember the special reminders I have of her.

Stage Four – Honoring the Memory

Month Three ◆ Day 5

I will try to accept that I will be reminded of him and that I will sometimes react with a smile and sometimes with a tear.

Month Three ◆ Day 6

Sometimes I want to run from reminders, but it may be better to think about them and to respect what they say to me.

Stage Four – Honoring the Memory

Month Three ◆ Day 7

An anniversary, birthday, or special memory day may be a hard time to stay focused; so on these days I will think only about the good things we shared.

_____

_____

_____

_____

Month Three ◆ Day 8

I am comforted to think that her presence is near.

_____

_____

_____

_____

Stage Four – Honoring the Memory

Month Three ♦ Day 9

When I am ready I will look at the photos I have and think about the joy we've shared.

Month Three ♦ Day 10

Other losses may bring back memories of this loss; I will try to embrace these memories and accept them as a part of nature.

Stage Four – Honoring the Memory

Month Three ◆ Day 11

Reminders show up in places I have never noticed before; I will accept them.

_____

_____

_____

_____

Month Three ◆ Day 12

A cloud may be shaped in a way that reminds me of my loved one. I shall try to define in words what it is.

_____

_____

_____

_____

Stage Four – Honoring the Memory

Month Three ♦ Day 13

This is what I loved about him. I am going to think of ways to incorporate this in my life.

_____

_____

_____

_____

Month Three ♦ Day 14

When I am looking at cards friends have sent me, I will tell myself it is okay to laugh and cry at the same time because words can stimulate mixed feelings.

_____

_____

_____

_____

Stage Four – Honoring the Memory

Month Three ♦ Day 15

As I move through this healing journey, I realize we have choices.

_____

_____

_____

_____

Month Three ♦ Day 16

I will hold the anniversary date of her death to reflect, but not to dwell.

_____

_____

_____

_____

Stage Four – Honoring the Memory

Month Three ◆ Day 17

As I sort through items belonging to him, I will linger on the memories they evoke.

_____
_____
_____
_____

Month Three ◆ Day 18

I am going to start a list here as to how I can honor her memory and create a suitable legacy.

_____
_____
_____
_____

Stage Four – Honoring the Memory

Month Three ♦ Day 19

I can still honor important dates (birthdays, holidays, anniversaries, family celebrations) we once shared.

_____

_____

_____

_____

Month Three ♦ Day 20

I will keep at least one candle to light in her memory on special occasions and when I personally feel the need.

_____

_____

_____

_____

Stage Four – Honoring the Memory

Month Three ◆ Day 21

I am learning to treasure each moment I have a happy thought about him.

_____

_____

_____

_____

Month Three ◆ Day 22

I realize now why people stop at cemeteries. I feel comfortable talking to her there and telling her how I miss her.

_____

_____

_____

_____

Stage Four – Honoring the Memory

Month Three ◆ Day 23

I realize now how good it was to have someone who cherished me. I will do the same for her memory.

_____

_____

_____

_____

Month Three ◆ Day 24

I will think about what I can preserve as something that represents who she was—perhaps a kindness to someone else or a representation of how she helped so many people.

_____

_____

_____

_____

Stage Four – Honoring the Memory

Month Three ♦ Day 25

I wonder if I can develop a trait in myself that I loved about her.

___

Month Three ♦ Day 26

I am going to plant a tree to symbolize the journey I am taking.

Stage Four – Honoring the Memory

Month Three ◆ Day 27

I will prepare a memory box for the special items that were important to him . . .

_____

_____

_____

_____

Month Three ◆ Day 28

I will choose one meaningful memento belonging to him and place it where I will see it every day.

_____

_____

_____

_____

Stage Four – Honoring the Memory

Month Three ♦ Day 29

I know now what is meant by keeping her memory alive in my heart and soul.

___

Month Three ♦ Day 30

By writing in this journal I have expressed my feelings for the one I loved for now and forever.

www.ingramcontent.com/pod-product-compliance
Lightning Source LLC
Chambersburg PA
CBHW061413090426

42742CB00023B/3458